On the Tip of My Tongue

A Mystery Fantasy for Children in Two Acts

by Austin O'Toole

A Samuel French Acting Edition

New York Hollywood London Toronto
SAMUELFRENCH.COM

Copyright © 1980 by Austin Michael O'Toole

ALL RIGHTS RESERVED

CAUTION: Professionals and amateurs are hereby warned that *ON THE TIP OF MY TONGUE* is subject to a Licensing Fee. It is fully protected under the copyright laws of the United States of America, the British Commonwealth, including Canada, and all other countries of the Copyright Union. All rights, including professional, amateur, motion picture, recitation, lecturing, public reading, radio broadcasting, television and the rights of translation into foreign languages are strictly reserved. In its present form the play is dedicated to the reading public only.

The amateur live stage performance rights to *ON THE TIP OF MY TONGUE* are controlled exclusively by Samuel French, Inc., and licensing arrangements and performance licenses must be secured well in advance of presentation. PLEASE NOTE that amateur Licensing Fees are set upon application in accordance with your producing circumstances. When applying for a licensing quotation and a performance license please give us the number of performances intended, dates of production, your seating capacity and admission fee. Licensing Fees are payable one week before the opening performance of the play to Samuel French, Inc., at 45 W. 25th Street, New York, NY 10010.

Licensing Fee of the required amount must be paid whether the play is presented for charity or gain and whether or not admission is charged.

Stock licensing fees quoted upon application to Samuel French, Inc.

For all other rights than those stipulated above, apply to: Samuel French, Inc.

Particular emphasis is laid on the question of amateur or professional readings, permission and terms for which must be secured in writing from Samuel French, Inc.

Copying from this book in whole or in part is strictly forbidden by law, and the right of performance is not transferable.

Whenever the play is produced the following notice must appear on all programs, printing and advertising for the play: "Produced by special arrangement with Samuel French, Inc."

Due authorship credit must be given on all programs, printing and advertising for the play.

No one shall commit or authorize any act or omission by which the copyright of, or the right to copyright, this play may be impaired.

No one shall make any changes in this play for the purpose of production.

Publication of this play does not imply availability for performance. Both amateurs and professionals considering a production are strongly advised in their own interests to apply to Samuel French, Inc., for written permission before starting rehearsals, advertising, or booking a theatre.

No part of this book may be reproduced, stored in a retrieval system, or transmitted in any form, by any means, now known or yet to be invented, including mechanical, electronic, photocopying, recording, videotaping, or otherwise, without the prior written permission of the publisher.

ISBN 978-0-573-65086-4   Printed in U.S.A.   #17631

CHARACTERS
(In speaking order)

Harry Smith—A young boy of no definite age. He is lively, rural in appearance and might easily pass for Tom Sawyer.

**Mrs. Smith—Harry's mother. Though simply dressed and somewhat plain she is at the same time quite beautiful. She has excellent carriage and projects great warmth. She is probably tall and slender.

*Hildy Smith—Harry's sister. Slightly older than Harry, she is pretty, a typical ingenue.

Ben Jordan—A boy of Harry's age, an enthusiastic though dusty sort who might easily pass for Huckleberry Finn.

Worry Bird—A hand puppet whose visible characteristics suggest a parrot. He is intelligent, funny, and a leader.

Owl Bird—A hand puppet. Though earthy and funny, he speaks in just slightly classic theatrical style. In his opinion, he is over-qualified for just about anything.

Dorothy of Kansas—The traditional ingenue from "The Wizard of Oz."

Witch of the West—The traditional wicked witch from "The Wizard of Oz." She wears a tall pointed hat and standard flowing black dress.

Injun Joe—The traditional villain from "The Adventures of Tom Sawyer." He does not wear American Indian garb; his clothing is standard midnineteenth-century street attire, though somewhat dishevelled.

**Double
*Double

**GLINDA, WITCH OF THE NORTH—The traditional good witch from "The Wizard of Oz." She is radiantly beautiful, dressed in a tiara and white flowing gown. She carries a wand.

WITCH FROM SNOW WHITE—The traditional witch from "Snow White and the Seven Dwarfs." She wears a standard flowing black dress with high collar and no hat.

*SNOW WHITE—The traditional ingenue from "Snow White and the Seven Dwarfs."

MISS ROTTENMEIER—The traditional middle-aged spinster from "Heidi."

HEIDI—The traditional ingenue from the story "Heidi."

KING MIDAS—The traditional king from "King Midas and the Golden Fleece."

PRINCESS TYRA—The traditional ingenue from "King Midas and the Golden Fleece."

**Double
 *Double

On The Tip of My Tongue

PROLOGUE

The Front Porch

Two or three steps lead up to the front porch where pieces of rustic summer furniture are arranged. A screen door separates the porch from the inside of the house, revealing a small vestibule. The porch setting should be a simple inset designed for a fast shift into Act One and the main body of the play.

The costumes and the attitudes reflect a time long past, perhaps the turn of the century.

The sun is bright; it is early afternoon. A young boy, HARRY SMITH, *is discovered painting the door frame. He dips his brush into an open paint can one or two times, dabs a final touch or two and steps back to admire his work.*

HARRY. (*His work finished, he calls into the house.*) It's all finished, Ma!
MRS. SMITH. (*From inside the house.*) I'll be right there. Don't go away!
HARRY. (*Sits on the porch steps and presses a lid onto the paint can.*) There, paint can. That'll be enough of you for a while. Now maybe I can go for a swim.
MRS. SMITH. (*Appears inside the screen door.*) What? Done already?

HARRY. Finished, Ma. It's all wet to the touch.

MRS. SMITH. (*Enters onto the porch as she speaks.*) You're finished when your mother *tells* you you're finished. (*She touches the wood here and there all about the porch, rubbing her fingers together.*) My goodness, you did it all. I must say that it looks very, very nice. You *can* work when you put your mind to it. (*She moves to the steps, sits beside* HARRY, *places her arm about his shoulders.*) I'm sorry that I scolded you this morning. Will you forgive me?

HARRY. Sure, Ma, but it's summertime and all the other kids are down by the swimming hole.

MRS. SMITH. I know they are, Harry, but it's different for us. You'll see that more and more as you grow older. Ever since the Good Lord took your father from us, the chores seem to grow bigger every week. The house needs so much attention and I need your help. I count on you more each day.

HARRY. Diane Willcmahagen had a picnic in the park yesterday afternoon and I couldn't even go. I was pulling weeds in the back yard.

MRS. SMITH. And the vegetable garden looks so much better for your hard work.

HARRY. Thanks, Ma.

MRS. SMITH. You're a great comfort to me, Harry, and you deserve a reward for all that. Tomorrow I'm going to let you do whatever you want to do, all day!

HARRY. Tomorrow! Aw, Ma, what about today? There's the whole afternoon left and everybody's down at the swimming hole.

MRS. SMITH. Not Lynn Boyleston. I happen to know that she's helping her mother clean house this very minute. Tomorrow, Harry. I want you to go to the grocery store this afternoon and then I want you to pick up some hardware.

HARRY. Aw, Ma, I feel like a prisoner.

Mrs. Smith. Harry, you're not to talk like that! I can't run this house by myself!

Harry. Why can't Hildy go to the store?

Mrs. Smith. Hildy's helping me prepare for the canning season. She does the household chores and she *doesn't* complain. (*Calls out.*) Hildy!

Hildy. (*From within the house.*) Yes, Mama.

Mrs. Smith. What do you need at the store? Did you finish the list?

Hildy. (*From within.*) Yes, Mama. I'll bring it to you.

Mrs. Smith. (*To* Harry.) She *doesn't* complain.

Harry. Naw, not when you're *around*.

Mrs. Smith. That will be enough, Harold.

Hildy. (*Enters onto the porch from the house.*) Here's the list, Mama. Groceries are at the top and hardware is at the bottom. I added a can of paint for the back porch.

Harry. Aaaaw!

Mrs. Smith. That's enough! Hurry along, now, before it clouds up. We're due for rain this afternoon and I don't want you caught.

Harry. That's as close to a swim as I'll get today.

Mrs. Smith. (*Has risen, is at the screen door where she turns toward* Harry.) Harry . . . you're right! (*Exits into the house.*)

Harry. (*To* Hildy.) I didn't know we had rats in the house.

Hildy. We don't.

Harry. Hildy, the rat.

Hildy. We can't let the house fall apart, can we?

Harry. I don't know why they named you Hildy.

Hildy. You have a better name?

Harry. Snow White. You're so *good*.

Hildy. Is that so! Well, you're so bad they should have named you Tom Sawyer!

HARRY. That ain't so bad. He got to go swimming and he didn't have a sister.

MRS. SMITH. (*Appears at the doorway.*) Harry, did I hear you say "ain't?"

HARRY. Aw, it just slipped out.

MRS. SMITH. You're not to use that word. "Isn't" isn't hard to say. You know better. Come, Hildy, I'm ready to make the beds. (*Exits into the house.*)

HILDY. (*Walks to the door, turns to* HARRY.) *Isn't* it a pretty day to go to the store! (*Exits into the house.*)

HARRY. (*Slumps forward, resting his head on his arms, on his knees.*) Aaaaw!

BEN. (*Enters after a moment, saunters toward the porch and* HARRY.) Hi, Harry. Thought I'd come by and see if you want to go swimming.

HARRY. (*Lifts his head, glares at* BEN.) I want to but I *ain't!*

BEN. Whew, look at that porch! That's pretty as a picket fence. Where'd you learn to paint like that?

HARRY. (*Through clenched teeth.*) Experience.

BEN. Well, that's something I never had to learn. Glad of it, too.

HARRY. You going swimming, Ben?

BEN. I'd like to but I shouldn't. Pa wants me to mow the lawn before it rains.

HARRY. I have to go for groceries and stop at the hardware store. That'll just about bring me to suppertime.

BEN. Somethin', ain't it. You look forward to vacation all winter long and when it comes all you get to do is work.

HARRY. Paintin'.

BEN. Mowin'.

HARRY. Weedin'.

BEN. Seedin'.

ON THE TIP OF MY TONGUE

HARRY. Wouldn't it be nice if grass would just stop growin'!

BEN. It never will. I got callouses on my hands big as a nickel.

HARRY. (*Looks at his outstretched palms.*) If I could put these dime-size in the bank, I'd be rich. Never have to work another day.

BEN. I swear I'm beginnin' to look forward to school.

HARRY. That's right. I never had to *paint* the school!

BEN. It's enough to make you want to run away.

HARRY. Wouldn't that be fine. Picnic all the time.

BEN. No baths. Just swimmin'.

HARRY. Nobody there to say you can't say "ain't." (*A pause, they look at each other, then speak together through locked jaws.*) Ain't!

BEN. (*Simultaneously.*) Ain't!

MRS. SMITH. (*Offstage.*) Harold!

HARRY. Sorry, Ma, it just slipped out again. (*To* BEN.) You see what I mean?

BEN. Ain't it awful.

HILDY. (*Enters from the house.*) Here's the list and the money. Mama says that you're not to dawdle.

HARRY. I'll dawdle if I want to dawdle. (*To* BEN.) Did you know we have a rat in the house?

BEN. Do tell! You better catch him. They nibble at your toes when you sleep.

HARRY. It *isn't* a him, it's a her.

BEN. (*Embarrassed.*) Oh. Well, I wouldn't know about that.

HILDY. Do you want me to tell Mama you called me a rat?

HARRY. All right. I'm going.

HILDY. And remember, don't dawdle. (*Exits into the house.*)

HARRY. So much for swimming, Ben. You see what I'm up against.

BEN. It's a sizzler to have a sister. Mine's the same.
HARRY. Were you serious just now?
BEN. Just when?
HARRY. Just now . . . about running away.
BEN. Sure. It's been on my mind all week long, though Pa hasn't given me much time to think about it.
HARRY. What's to think about? We each pack some food and a blanket and strike out past the river.
BEN. I suppose we could . . . for a little while.
HARRY. A little while? Come on, Ben.
BEN. Well, I don't want to get into any trouble with Pa.
HARRY. What kind of trouble can you get into if you ain't at home?
BEN. You mean you're thinking of running away . . . overnight?
HARRY. Well, sure.
BEN. I was thinking more like running away in the morning and getting back in plenty of time to wash up for supper.
HARRY. That ain't running away, Ben, that's going on a picnic and I ain't allowed to do even that. Running away is different. Running away is overnight . . . at least!
BEN. Overnight. That could bring on a licking like I never dreamed of.
HARRY. Don't back down now, Ben. It's your idea.
BEN. Half the credit's yours just for how fast you jumped on it.
HARRY. All right, I'll take half the credit if it makes you feel better.
BEN. Overnight . . .
MRS. SMITH. (*Appears in the doorway.*) Haven't you gone yet, Harry?
BEN. Hello, Mrs. Smith.

Mrs. Smith. Ben, Harry has chores to do. Run along home now. I'm sure your folks have chores for you, too. (*Exits.*)

Ben. (*Convinced.*) When do we go?

Harry. Tomorrow morning. Ma gave me the day off. They won't miss us 'til nightfall and by then we'll be miles off in the woods.

Ben. I'll meet you down by the swimming hole right after breakfast. Bring plenty of food and a good blanket. I'll do the same.

Harry. I'll be there. Get a good night's sleep. We're gonna need all our strength.

Ben. This has probably fixed me for sleep, all right, but I'll try.

Harry. Go on, now, I'll see you in the morning.

Ben. Happy day, no more cares! (*Starts to exit, turns back.*) Right after breakfast. Eat a big one.

Harry. I will. You, too. (Ben *exits as they wave to each other.* Harry *calls into the house.*) Ma, I'm ready to go to the store now . . . (*Aside, to himself.*) even if I ain't!

CURTAIN

ACT ONE

A Clearing in the Woods.

The setting may be quite simple or as full as facilities allow.

Ideally, the stage should be bursting with lush greenery, trees, hedgerows, knolls and flowers, all arranged on platforms at various levels for a more dynamic performance. Simpler design might be enhanced by imaginative lighting, projections and silhouettes.

The setting is unoccupied for a moment or two after the curtain rises. We are allowed to feel the isolation, to hear the birds. Music might underscore the mood and fade slowly as BEN *enters, obviously tired.*

BEN. (*Enters, looks about. He carries a knapsack, slowly crosses the clearing to a far side and sinks to the ground.*) This way, Harry.

HARRY. (*Enters, dragging his knapsack behind. He sinks to the ground even before crossing the clearing.*) Don't go ahead so far, Ben. We might lose sight of each other.

BEN. Harry, I can't go much further.

HARRY. I can't keep my eyes open. My, what a nice spot. It seems as good a place as any to stop for the night.

BEN. That's what I was thinking.

HARRY. (*After a moment.*) I'm hungry as a bear in springtime.

BEN. Me, too. (*Opens his knapsack, shuffles its contents.*) Oh, my, look at this.

HARRY. (*Rises, drags his knapsack along the ground and sits near* BEN.) What is it?

BEN. All my vegetables are shrivelled up.

HARRY. They're all wrinkled. Whew! They don't smell very good, either!

BEN. We should have had them on ice.

HARRY. Sure, but how could we carry that much weight? Besides, it's been so hot we wouldn't have had even a sliver of ice after our first mile out.

BEN. (*After a moment.*) How far do you think we've come?

HARRY. Oh, miles and miles. We passed over the river about noon and that's five miles from town. We've travelled that much again, at least.

BEN. What'll we eat?

HARRY. The apples still look good. I brought a lot of apples. (*Offers one to* BEN.) Here. We'll find berries and fruit trees in the morning. There must be plenty of food growing free.

BEN. Right now I can't tell if I'm hungry or tired. (*After a moment.*) I think I'm tired. I'll save my apple for later.

HARRY. I will, too.

BEN. This place is farther into the woods than I've ever been or even heard of.

HARRY. I know. Soon as we passed the old tree stump some yards back it seemed even the colors changed. It even smells different. Kinda nice, except for the wrinkled vegetables you brought along.

BEN. Well, how was I to know? I never ran away before, not for overnight, anyway.

HARRY. Raw beets for dinner wouldn't be so good even if they *didn't* have wrinkles.

BEN. It's starting to turn dark. I bet it's seven o'clock by now, town time.

HARRY. It's hard to tell here in the woods, there's so little sky.

BEN. (*After a moment.*) Do you suppose they're looking for us?

HARRY. I suppose so, but they'll never find us in here, 'specially at night.

BEN. I hope they don't fret too much. I never did think of that.

HARRY. Me, either. I know Ma won't sleep a wink tonight and I never gave it a thought.

BEN. Maybe *she* won't, but *I* will! I haven't been so weary since final exams. (*Begins to unfold his blanket.*)

HARRY. The last time I was this tired was the fifth of July. I could have slept 'til noon but Ma got me up at six to wash the windows. (*Both are arranging sleeping areas, pulling blankets about them as they speak.*)

BEN. Well, I ain't seen a window since we crossed the river, so that's a good sign.

HARRY. I guess Hildy will have to spruce the back porch herself, she was so anxious to buy that paint. I'd like to be a bird watching *that* from nearby. (BEN *snores.*) Ben. Ben!

BEN. (*Jumps, alarmed.*) Who is it? Who's there!

HARRY. Just me.

BEN. Harry? Oh, you scared me. Guess I fell asleep.

HARRY. Sounded like a locust tree, you snored so loud.

BEN. Sure is nice and cool in here. Good night for sleeping. Pa says we're headed for an early fall. Reckon he's right. (HARRY *snores.*) You asleep? Harry. Harry!

HARRY. (*Jumps.*) Who goes there?

BEN. It's me, Harry. Ben.
HARRY. Oh, I fell into a dream. There was animals.
BEN. Get some sleep.
HARRY. What do you think I was doing?
BEN. I mean some good sleep, not just a doze.
HARRY. I'll try if you'll hush and let me.
BEN. (*After a pause and some shifting under his blanket.*) Harry, are you awake?
HARRY. Just barely, 'til now.
BEN. Do wild animals live in these woods?
HARRY. Don't know.
BEN. If they do, do you think they'll smell us?
HARRY. If they don't smell us, they'll whiff them vegetables.
BEN. Pa says there used to be grizzlies in here. Think we'll see a grizzly?
HARRY. The grizzlies all moved out since the town grew larger. They don't like people.
BEN. Not unless they're hungry. Then they ain't too particular.
HARRY. There ain't no grizzlies. (*Both pull their covers up. A pause and* HARRY *continues.*) Snakes, yes, but no grizzlies.
BEN. Snakes!
HARRY. (*Laughs.*) Haha! I thought that would get you. There ain't no snakes, either. I heard that somewhere. Now go to sleep.
BEN. (*After a pause.*) Hyenas, but no snakes. (*Chuckles.*)
HARRY. Gorillas, but no hyenas. (*Both laugh, then silence. They are asleep. Forest sounds are heard. As the sounds build the lighting changes to different hues and intensities, giving the clearing a look of even greater fantasy. The sounds diminish slowly until they are barely heard. A large bird pops up at the top of a hedgerow. While we are allowed time to observe the*

bird, we see him routinely observing and checking his habitat. Suddenly, the bird spies the sleeping intruders.)

WORRY. What! What's this? Owl!

OWL. *(Pops up in another part of the clearing.)* Hoot! Roused from a deep sleep before its time is spent!

WORRY. Stow the Shakespeare! This is serious.

OWL. Zounds!

WORRY. Who are these two? Do you know them? They're not on my list.

OWL. Lo and behold, I know not.

WORRY. I know not, too. I mean I don't know who they are. They were definitely not invited.

OWL. Is thee certain? They appear somewhat familiar, methinks, and in truth.

WORRY. Will you stick to the point, Owl? We all know you can read, *and* write, *and* sound like a talking encyclopedia.

OWL. Sooth, what fury!

WORRY. Fury, my feathers! Getting a straight answer out of you is like learning the Greek alphabet . . . backwards!

OWL. Sticks and stones may break my tones, but words will ne'er forsake me.

WORRY. Just a simple answer, Owl. Do you know these two?

OWL. A scruffy pair, from no literary masterpiece, and yet would seemst to know them.

WORRY. Would seemst . . . there, you have me doing it. It seems I know them, too.

OWL. Perchance we shouldst worry for them.

WORRY. Good idea. Obviously, they're in some kind of trouble.

OWL. A quagmire, a billowing bog of turmoil, me feels.

WORRY. Promise me something, Owl.
OWL. Sooth?
WORRY. Don't ever enter a contest in fifty words or less.
OWL. Rumpled rudeness!
WORRY. Shall we wake them? We have to *know*.
OWL. Hoot, mon.
WORRY. Are you ready?
OWL. Hoot!
WORRY. One, two, three . . . (WORRY *and* OWL *screech loudly, waking the boys.*)
HARRY. Ben!
BEN. (*Simultaneously.*) Harry!
HARRY and BEN. (*Together.*) I heard something!
WORRY. You heard me.
HARRY. Who's there?
WORRY. Over here.
BEN. It's a bird.
WORRY. Plain as the beak on my face. They're *not* dummies, Owl.
OWL. Hoot, mon.
HARRY. Another bird.
BEN. And they both talk!
HARRY. (*To* WORRY.) Do you birds talk?
WORRY. I talk. He blusters.
OWL. Conjecture, me lads, forsooth. Four score and twenty years ago, at the very least!
HARRY. (*To* WORRY.) He blusters.
WORRY. (*To* HARRY.) What brings you here? Who invited you?
HARRY. Oh, we weren't invited.
OWL. I told you, a scruffy pair. No couth!
HARRY. We ran away from home and chose this place for a night's sleep.
WORRY. Ran away from home? Mark that one, Owl. It's a clue.

Owl. We'll track it for its worth.

Worry. Do you have names?

Harry. Oh, yes. I'm Harry Smith. This is Ben Jordan.

Worry. I am Worry Bird, and that's my cousin, Owl Bird.

Owl. I have a degree!

Worry. A degree of conceit! (*Laughs.*)

Owl. Hoot! Meandering succotash for a brain, that one. He's worried himself into a lassitude.

Harry. (*To* Worry.) Are you really the famous Worry Bird?

Worry. Ah, yes, alas and alack.

Owl. Well put, cousin. You'll get the hang of it if you don't hang first! (*He laughs.*)

Worry. (*To* Harry.) But who *are* you?

Harry. I told you. I'm Harry, this is . . .

Worry. (*Interrupting.*) I know, I know, Harry and Ben, but those aren't your real names. I don't know a single story about a Harry and Ben. You're using those names to hide your true identity. (*Upstage, running through two or three times,* Dorothy of Kansas *is seen. Chasing at her heels is the* Wicked Witch of the West. *During the chase, the dialogue is heard.*)

Dorothy. No, no, no!

Witch of the West. Ahaaa!

Dorothy. Please let me go home!

Witch of the West. Never! I'll get you my little pretty!

Dorothy. But we did what you asked of us!

Witch of the West. And I'll get your little dog, too! (*They exit.*)

Harry. Who were those people?

Worry. Those were two reasons why you should get out of here before it's too late.

Owl. Post haste! You weren't invited!

Harry. I've seen them somewhere.

WORRY. Most likely, but we mustn't tell. They might find out who they are.

BEN. You mean they don't know?

WORRY. That's right, not any more than you know who you are.

HARRY. But we do know who we are. This is . . .

WORRY. Oh, not again! Harry and Ben. It makes a good story.

OWL. And not the least bit interesting, so far. A dime novel, to be sure.

HARRY. What's going on here? I don't understand anything you say.

OWL. You need a degree. Of enlightenment.

HARRY. I'll try to explain. We *know* who we are, Harry Smith and Ben Jordan. We ran away and came here by accident.

BEN. It's summer vacation and all we do is work. We left home to swim and picnic. Just yesterday I had to mow the lawn. Pa wanted me to finish it today.

HARRY. And I had to weed the garden and paint the porch.

OWL. Paint! Paint the porch? That rings a bell!

WORRY. Ding-a-ling!

OWL. Worry, what literature . . . what story, if you will . . . contains two boys who run away? Further I ask, what story tells of painting a porch or similar object?

WORRY. It's on the tip of my beak. It does ring a bell.

OWL. Ding-a-ling! However, your thinking and mine are Mississippi Rivers apart. Never the twain shall meet.

WORRY. Twain!

OWL. Twain! Chugga, chugga, chugga! Toot, toot! The Adventures of Tom Sawyer! (*To* HARRY.) *You* are Tom Sawyer!

HARRY. No!

WORRY. (*To* BEN.) And *you* are Huckleberry Finn!

BEN. No, I'm Ben Jordan! (INJUN JOE *leaps from the bushes with a great shout.* HARRY *and* BEN *are terrified as he approaches them slowly, menacingly. He inches toward* HARRY *who retreats as* BEN *moves to one side. Finally,* INJUN JOE *stops.*)

INJUN JOE. You tell me what you saw last night in the graveyard.

HARRY. Graveyard? I wasn't in the graveyard last night.

INJUN JOE. You always say that, always the same, every time someone reads the book.

HARRY. Honest! I wasn't in the graveyard. Who are you?

INJUN JOE. You know me. I know you, *Tom.*

HARRY. Tom? No, I'm Harry.

INJUN JOE. You never been Harry. You always been Tom.

HARRY. You're thinking of somebody else.

INJUN JOE. That not what you're supposed to say. You supposed to say, "I wasn't in the graveyard last night. I don't remember how I left my dead cat behind because of the terrible thing I saw." Now, say it right.

HARRY. I don't know what you're talking about! I don't know what *anybody* is talking about! (BEN *has inched behind* INJUN JOE, *slaps him on the back and shouts. Stunned,* INJUN JOE *runs off.*)

WORRY. (*To* BEN.) That's good, Huckleberry, you're doing it right. Just like the book.

BEN. What book?

WORRY. Wake up. Wake up before it's too late. (*Drops from view.*)

BEN. Wake up? But I *am* awake!

OWL. Wake up and wash the windows.

HARRY. What windows? This is a forest.

OWL. The windows are there. They'll need washing

ACT I   ON THE TIP OF MY TONGUE   21

soon. Find them. We're going to worry about you boys. Wake up before it's too late. (*Drops from view.*)

HARRY. (*Looks for the birds.*) Where did they go?

BEN. They just disappeared. They're not here.

HARRY. What's going on here, Ben?

BEN. I don't understand.

HARRY. Why does everybody think that I'm Tom Sawyer?

INJUN JOE. (*Appears Upstage, high above the boys on a parapet.*) Tom Sawyer, you keep what you know to yourself. I keep my eye on you . . . wherever you go! (*Exits.*)

HARRY. Lordy, I wish I was home.

BEN. Me, too.

HARRY. They're not very friendly, are they.

BEN. (*Begins to fold his blanket, gather the knapsacks.*) So much for sleep. Harry, you can run away if you want to but I'm going home.

HARRY. I'll go with you. (*Gathers his goods, helps* BEN *fold the blankets. When they are packed,* BEN *speaks.*)

BEN. You ready?

HARRY. Ready, and not a minute too soon. (*They start out. After a moment or two* HARRY *speaks.*) The pathway is closed off. I can't find the way.

BEN. Me, either. It looks different somehow.

HARRY. (*Crosses to another area.*) Try over here.

BEN. No, that ain't the way.

HARRY. There's no way out!

BEN. What'll we do, Harry? (*On an Upstage parapet a warm light grows. As the boys become aware of the glow they back off from its brilliance.*) What is it?

HARRY. Don't know.

GLINDA, WITCH OF THE NORTH. (*Steps gently into the brilliant light. She is radiantly beautiful, dressed*

in a tiara and white flowing gown. She carries a wand.)
I'm afraid I can't let you go just yet.

BEN. Who are you?

GLINDA. I can't say.

HARRY. Don't you know?

GLINDA. Oh, yes, I know, but I mustn't tell. You may call me Gwin, for now.

HARRY. You *know* who you are and still you can't tell us?

GLINDA. None of us must tell until it is time.

HARRY. When will that be?

GLINDA. At the beginning of the trial.

HARRY. Who is on trial?

GLINDA. We are all on trial in one way or another.

BEN. Are we on trial?

GLINDA. Oh, yes, especially you two. (*The light fades and* GLINDA *steps down to join them. At her approach the boys back off.*) Don't be afraid. I won't harm you.

HARRY. Every time we ask a question nobody seems to know the answer.

BEN. And if they know, they won't tell.

HARRY. Or can't tell. And everybody keeps mistaking us for Tom Sawyer and Huckleberry Finn.

GLINDA. Well, *are* you?

HARRY. (*Turns away in anguish.*) Aaaaw!

BEN. (*Turns simultaneuosly.*) Aaaaw!

GLINDA. I know how puzzling it all must seem. (*Seats herself on a knoll.*) Come. Sit beside me and I'll explain it to you. Come, I won't bite, I promise.

BEN. You're allowed to tell us?

GLINDA. As much as I can, yes. Come, sit. (*The boys sit on either side of her.*) Once a year, all the villains in all the stories of the world are called together in this glen.

BEN. What's a villain?

GLINDA. Those are the bad people in the stories, the people who bring harm or try to bring harm to others.

HARRY. You mean like Jack the Ripper or Lady Macbeth?

GLINDA. Well, no, not exactly.

HARRY. Ma told me about them.

GLINDA. When I say that all the villains come here, that's true. Unfortunately, there are so many that we are forced to hold many trials for just a few at a time. You won't see Lady Macbeth or Jack the Ripper at this trial, but you might recognize some of the others.

HARRY. I think I know *one* already.

BEN. What happens at the trial?

GLINDA. The good people in the stories, the ones who are harmed by the villains, come here also. They try to show the bad people how useless it is to be so bad. Everytime someone opens a book, each story happens all over again, as though for the first time. We keep hoping that some day the stories will change, that the bad ones might turn to good instead of evil.

BEN. Has any villain ever done that?

GLINDA. Not as far as we know but we'll never stop trying.

HARRY. Isn't it dangerous to have so many villains in one place?

GLINDA. It is very, very dangerous and we try to control that. We never let them know who they are until the trial.

HARRY. How do you do that?

GLINDA. There are just two times when a villain truly knows who he is . . . when someone reads his story and he is forced to act out his role, and when we take roll call at the trial.

HARRY. So we're safe from them at any other time.

GLINDA. No, we definitely are not. These are very bad people, you must remember. The fact that they don't always know who they are doesn't alter their strong desire to do great harm.

BEN. Who runs the trial?

GLINDA. The Worry Bird thought of the trial many years ago and he is the presiding officer. Owl Bird is his legal advisor and I am the hostess. Poor Worry has so much to worry about.

BEN. Is that how he got his name?

GLINDA. (*Pats him on the head.*) Yes.

HARRY. Why are we on trial? We're not villains.

GLINDA. If you turn out to be Tom Sawyer and Huckleberry Finn you are certainly not villains, it's true. But Tom and Huck are always getting into trouble. It would be nice if we could get them to change their ways, just a little.

HARRY. And if we can prove that we really are Harry and Ben, will we be on trial then?

GLINDA. Oh, yes, indeed. If you truly are Harry and Ben you will be part of a brand new story never told before. Not until the story is over will we know whether you are good boys or bad boys. You could turn out to be more troublesome than Tom and Huck.

BEN. But we're not part of a story. We really aren't.

GLINDA. Oh, yes, you really are. We are all part of a story and yours is being written at this very moment.

BEN. Who's writing it?

GLINDA. Someone who probably cares for you very much, though you're not likely to know that person.

HARRY. Are you part of a story?

GLINDA. Yes, everyone is. Everyone here and everyone out there, in all the world. Everyone you know is part of a story.

BEN. Will we have to come back here every year?

GLINDA. Only if you turn out to be bad, or if you encounter a villain who does you great harm. If your story is carefully written you will never, never have to come back to the glen.

ACT I ON THE TIP OF MY TONGUE 25

BEN. What is our story called?

GLINDA. We don't know that yet. We won't know until after the trial. Now, I have a surprise for you. All of the good characters from the stories represented at this trial are here to meet you.

BEN. Will we know their names?

GLINDA. Not yet. The names could be overheard by the villains and they would know precisely who they are. That would give them strength. We wouldn't want that to happen.

HARRY. No.

GLINDA. (*Rises, claps her hands together.*) Come out, wherever you are!

(*One at a time, from all parts of the glen,* DOROTHY OF KANSAS, HEIDI, SNOW WHITE, *and* PRINCESS TYRA *position themselves on the knolls, ramps and parapets. When all have entered and are standing quite still,* GLINDA *speaks.*)

GLINDA. Do you know any of them?

HARRY. I think I do.

GLINDA. Remember, don't speak their names.

HARRY. May I whisper one to you?

GLINDA. Yes, but very softly. (HARRY *points to one and whispers into* GLINDA'S *ear.*) That's right, Harry.

HARRY. It's one of my favorite stories.

GLINDA. Now you'll want to read it again.

BEN. (*Suddenly, forgetting his warning.*) I know! I know that one! It's Snow White!

WITCH FROM SNOW WHITE. (*Bursts onto the stage into a green spotlight, cackling in great delight.*) Aaaaha! I thought so and now I have it for certain. She *is* Snow White! I heard the name! I know how to deal with her. I always have. (*Moves to* SNOW WHITE.) Take this apple, dearie, it's such a beauty!

GLINDA. (*To* SNOW WHITE.) Don't do it! (*To the* WITCH.) Stand back from her! I'm in charge here!

WITCH FROM SNOW WHITE. You think you are but I can play your little game, too!

GLINDA. We're not playing a game. This is the Grand Court of the Worry Bird and you have no power here.

WITCH FROM SNOW WHITE. Can you be so sure? Do I detect a little hesitancy, a glimmer of fear in your eye? Have your little plans gone astray?

GLINDA. Try as you may, you can't shake my confidence. You haven't the power to overcome the good that surrounds you here.

WITCH FROM SNOW WHITE. Power! Ah, that's the key word. (*She has moved to the knoll where* GLINDA *had been seated. She picks up the wand that* GLINDA *left behind.*) Is this your power?

GLINDA. My wand! Give me that!

WITCH FROM SNOW WHITE. What sort of fool do you take me for? Give it to you? I should say not! Not for a bushel of my sweetest apples. This wand is your power and now it's mine!

GLINDA. How could I have been so careless!

BEN. It's all my fault.

WITCH FROM SNOW WHITE. That's right, lad. Your story isn't going so well now, is it? The wand is mine, you are mine . . . (*To the entire assemblage.*) you are all mine! Villains! Enter! Take them!

(*At once the villains appear.* THE WICKED WITCH OF THE WEST *crosses to* DOROTHY OF KANSAS; KING MIDAS *crosses to* PRINCESS TYRA; MISS ROTTENMEIER *crosses to* HEIDI; THE WITCH FROM SNOW WHITE *stands near* SNOW WHITE; INJUN JOE *enters and overpowers* HARRY *and* BEN.)

GLINDA. Villains! This will not go well for you!

WITCH FROM SNOW WHITE. Ahaaa! That's good! (*To* GLINDA.) Or should I say that's bad, very bad.

GLINDA. You must stop this immediately!

WITCH FROM SNOW WHITE. Stop? Oh, no, this is just the beginning. Take her! (*The* WICKED WITCH OF THE WEST *pulls* DOROTHY OF KANSAS *with her as she grasps* GLINDA's *arm.*) Now, my lovely, watch this. You've seen it a thousand times before, but observe once more. (*Turns from* GLINDA, *moves toward* SNOW WHITE.) And now Snow White, take the lovely gift, the beautiful apple.

GLINDA. Snow White!

WITCH FROM SNOW WHITE. Silence! (*To* SNOW WHITE.) See how red, how lovely. (SNOW WHITE *takes the apple innocently.*) No, try this side. It's so much nicer. (SNOW WHITE *bites the apple as all watch helplessly. She staggers, reels, slumps to the ground center.*) Ahaaa! We'll see who's on trial here, won't we! We'll see!

CURTAIN

ACT TWO

A Clearing in the Woods.

At rise the clearing is occupied by WORRY *and* OWL *who sit atop their hedgerows, now housed in separate cages.* SNOW WHITE *is seen sleeping far Upstage.*

OWL. Zounds! Lo and behold! Methinks there's been a change. Can these be cages surround us?
WORRY. Definitely cages.
OWL. It bodes ill tidings. 'Tis darkness at noon and a moon for the misbegotten.
WORRY. And besides that, we're in trouble.
OWL. Hoot.
WORRY. I remember falling asleep. That's all. I woke up in this one room apartment.
OWL. What doth it mean?
WORRY. I know not. I mean, I don't know.
OWL. A mystery to be unravelled.
WORRY. What was that?
OWL. I hear nothing.
WORRY. Someone's coming. Hide!
OWL. Can'tst hide, cousin, no place to go.
WITCH FROM SNOW WHITE. (*Enters.*) Aha! My birds of a feather! Do you like your new cages?
OWL. Midnight rainbow, look who's here.
WORRY. It's the Witch from Snow White!
WITCH FROM SNOW WHITE. That's right, it is I, the fairest of them all.
OWL. Best to take another look.
WITCH FROM SNOW WHITE. Watch your tongue, Owl!
OWL. No small feat.

WITCH FROM SNOW WHITE. Were you surprised to wake up in your little rooms?
WORRY. When do we eat?
WITCH FROM SNOW WHITE. Oh, Worry want a cracker? I don't have any. How about an apple? Ha-haa!
WORRY. I'm on a diet. Suddenly.
OWL. Hoot. Must tighten the belt.
WITCH FROM SNOW WHITE. I should say, but we have more "weighty" matters to discuss here.
WORRY. That's what worries me.
WITCH FROM SNOW WHITE. And well it should. You are about to stand trial, Worry Bird. Do you consider that weighty?
WORRY. Food for thought . . .
OWL. . . . and cause for alarm.
WORRY. Ring-a-ding!
WITCH FROM SNOW WHITE. That will be quite enough! Remember your place, my little prisoner.
OWL. Gulp!
WITCH FROM SNOW WHITE. What was that?
OWL. Gulp! Just a *little* gulp.
WITCH FROM SNOW WHITE. It had better be. There will be no more impertinence, is that understood?
WORRY. Gulp!
WITCH FROM SNOW WHITE. What!!
WORRY. No! I mean yes! Yes, there will be no more impertinence! No!
WITCH FROM SNOW WHITE. You'd better start to worry, bird, now that the shoe is on the other claw.
OWL. Wry.
WITCH FROM SNOW WHITE. Eh?
OWL. Bologna on rye! Hold the mustard!
WITCH FROM SNOW WHITE. No more from you!
OWL. You're probably right.
WITCH FROM SNOW WHITE. Prepare to meet your

jury. (*Claps her hands.*) Villains! Enter! (*The villains file in, arranging themselves as in a jury box at one side of the clearing.*) They'll treat you fairly, I'm sure. Don't you agree? (*To* OWL.) Well, don't you?

OWL. Fair as a case of measles.

WITCH FROM SNOW WHITE. You'll beg for measles before they're through and then you'll have me to deal with. (*Calls off.*) Injun Joe! (INJUN JOE *enters.*) Bring me the boys! (*He exits.*) You see, my birdies, I have gained control of Gwin's magic wand, the only power I had to fear. And now she is my captive. (INJUN JOE *returns with* HARRY *and* BEN.) Aha! Here they are now, our mystery guests. This court will come to order. Let the trial begin!

WITCH OF THE WEST. (*From the "jury box."*) We need Gwin to take the stand.

WITCH FROM SNOW WHITE. Then fetch her! And be quick about it!

WITCH OF THE WEST. Watch your tone with me.

WITCH FROM SNOW WHITE. (*Raises the wand, threateningly.*) Who is the fairest in all the land?

WITCH OF THE WEST. You are. (*Exits.*)

WITCH FROM SNOW WHITE. I want you all to remember who's the fairest here. Well, do you?

VILLAINS. (*All, in unison.*) Snow White, your ugliness! (*They laugh uproariously, slapping each other about.*)

WITCH FROM SNOW WHITE. Order! Order, I say! So long as I have Gwin's magic wand, you'd best watch your tongues. (*The* VILLAINS *stick out, stare at each other's tongues. The* WITCH *does not see them as she continues.*) Who is the fairest in the land?

VILLAINS. (*All, in unison.*) We guess you are, your lowness. We mean your highness!

WITCH FROM SNOW WHITE. That's better.

WITCH OF THE WEST. (*Enters, leads* GLINDA *to*

center.) Here she is, your prettiness. (*To* GLINDA.) That's nice perfume. Where did you get it?

WITCH FROM SNOW WHITE. *Will* you stop and get down to business? Take your place!

WITCH OF THE WEST. Sorry. But it is nice perfume. (*Takes her place with the "jury."*)

WITCH FROM SNOW WHITE. If I hear one more word about perfume here today I'll turn you into a grubworm.

WITCH OF THE WEST. (*Loud whisper to* GLINDA.) Talk to you later.

WITCH FROM SNOW WHITE. Court will come to order, again!

VILLAINS. (*All, in unison.*) Order in the court, if you please, and don't sneeze. (*All sneeze repeatedly.* THE WITCH FROM SNOW WHITE *stares them into silence.*)

WITCH FROM SNOW WHITE. Will you pay attention! The next one who speaks out of turn gets the measles.

OWL. Hoot.

WITCH FROM SNOW WHITE. A pox on you! Wand, give him the measles!

GLINDA. Nonsense, you can't give measles to a bird.

WITCH FROM SNOW WHITE. Will you be quiet? You and your perfume started all this.

VILLAINS. (*All, in unison.*) Sure smells good. Where did you get that stuff?

WITCH FROM SNOW WHITE. Aaaah!

WITCH OF THE WEST. (*To* GLINDA.) Talk to you later.

WITCH FROM SNOW WHITE. (*Forcing the trial.*) The boys we see before us . . . are you listening? (*The* VILLAINS *snore.*) The boys we see before us have been identified. Injun Joe, you have the floor.

VILLAINS. (*All, in unison.*) Pick it up, Joe. (*All laugh, slap each other about.* THE WITCH FROM SNOW WHITE *glares them into silence.*)

WITCH FROM SNOW WHITE. Injun Joe, your statement.

INJUN JOE. No statement. No money in the bank.

WITCH FROM SNOW WHITE. Who are these boys!!

INJUN JOE. Oh, I know them. This one Tom Sawyer. This one Huckleberry Finn.

WITCH FROM SNOW WHITE. (*To* HARRY.) And are you Tom Sawyer?

HARRY. No!

WITCH FROM SNOW WHITE. And are you Huckleberry Finn?

BEN. My name's Ben Jordan!

WITCH FROM SNOW WHITE. Yes or no!

BEN. No!

WITCH FROM SNOW WHITE. You lie. You're using false names to cover your true identity. Villains! What is your verdict?

VILLAINS. (*All, in unison.*) String 'em up!

WITCH FROM SNOW WHITE. No, no, no! I want a verdict. I didn't ask you to sentence them.

VILLAINS. (*All, in unison.*) Sentence. A noun and a verb sprinkled with other goodies.

WITCH FROM SNOW WHITE. Are they guilty or not guilty?

VILLAINS. (*All, in unison.*) Oh! Guilty! String 'em up!

WITCH FROM SNOW WHITE. Guilty! Injun Joe, step aside and hold the boys. Gwin, take the stand.

VILLAINS. (*All, in unison.*) Pick it up, Gwin. (GLINDA *moves center.*)

WITCH FROM SNOW WHITE. Good. I've waited a long time to see you there. Now you know how it is to have the shoe on the other claw. Foot! Do you plead innocent or guilty?

GLINDA. Innocent. Definitely innocent.

WITCH FROM SNOW WHITE. (*To the "jury."*) Guilty or innocent?

VILLAINS. (*All, in unison.*) Guilty. String her up!

GLINDA. This is no trial. You ask if I am innocent or guilty. What am I accused of? Where are your legal papers? Where is my defense attorney?

WITCH FROM SNOW WHITE. I'll ask the questions!

VILLAINS. (*All, in unison.*) Go ahead, you've got the floor.

WITCH FROM SNOW WHITE. Enough! (*To* GLINDA.) May I remind you that you are the prisoner. You do not make the rules. Before this day has ended I will feed you to the birds.

WORRY. Ugh!

WITCH FROM SNOW WHITE. (*To* WORRY.) And you to the hawks! (*Points a finger into his cage.* WORRY *bites her, she reels back, dropping the wand.*) Aaaah! (HARRY *leaps forward toward the wand.* INJUN JOE *pursues him, fails to catch him after one or two close encounters.* HARRY *manages to elude* INJUN JOE *and struggles to reach* GLINDA. *At last* HARRY *delivers the wand to her.*)

GLINDA. (*Holding the wand high.*) Stop! Everyone! Where you are!

VILLAINS. (*All, in unison, point to* THE WITCH FROM SNOW WHITE.) Now you've done it.

GLINDA. Good work, Worry. You've saved the day.

WORRY. Tom Sawyer saved the day. I only bit her.

HARRY. Please, I'm not Tom Sawyer. How can I prove that?

GLINDA. Perhaps you already have. We'll see. Now this court *will* come to order. First, I will waken Snow White from her spell. (*She moves to the sleeping* SNOW WHITE, *touches the wand to her forehead.* SNOW WHITE *stretches, sits up and yawns.*)

SNOW WHITE. I feel weak. What's happened to me?

GLINDA. The same as always, I'm afraid, but you're safe now. Injun Joe, remove the cages. (INJUN JOE *lifts the cages from the hedgerows.*) Villains, you no longer have power. You are under control. I want you to move just outside the clearing until we call for you. Boys, watch them. They cannot harm you now. (*The* VILLAINS *exit, followed by* HARRY *and* BEN *who help* SNOW WHITE *off.*) The court is yours once more, Worry. Shall we begin?

WORRY. Let the trumpets sound. (*Trumpets peel.*) Hear ye, hear ye! The Grand Court of the Worry Bird, assisted by his cousin Owl . . .

OWL. Hear ye.

WORRY. . . . and the talented and lovely Gwin, will now come to order. Roll call!

GLINDA. I shall now read aloud the titles of five stories, followed by the name of its hero or heroine, followed by the name of its villain. When your name is called, please enter and take your place. Can you hear me?

ALL. (*Off.*) We hear you.

GLINDA. From the beautiful tale The Adventures of Heidi, Heidi . . . (HEIDI *enters, takes her place.*)

WORRY. (*Quietly.*) Hurray.

GLINDA. Miss Rottenmeier. (MISS ROTTENMEIER *enters.*)

WORRY. (*Quietly.*) Boo.

GLINDA. From King Midas and the Golden Fleece, Princess Tyra . . . (TYRA *enters,* HEIDI *applauds politely.*) King Midas. (KING MIDAS *enters.*)

OWL and WORRY. (*Hiss the villain.*) Pssss.

GLINDA. From Snow White and the Seven Dwarfs, Snow White . . . (*She enters to applause.*) and the Witch from Snow White. (*Enters to hisses.*) From the Wizard of Oz, Dorothy of Kansas . . . (*Enters to applause.*) and the Wicked Witch of the West. (*Enters to hisses.*)

WITCH OF THE WEST. (*To* GLINDA.) I'll get you for this.

GLINDA. Begone! You have no power here! (*Reads on.*) And, from Mark Twain's Adventures of Tom Sawyer, Tom Sawyer . . . (HARRY *enters, shrugs, takes his place.*) Huckleberry Finn . . . (BEN *enters, shrugs, takes his place.*) and finally, Injun Joe. (*Enters to hisses.*) There! We are all in our places and ready for the trial to begin. Are there any questions?

HARRY. Excuse me. You've named everyone here but we don't know who you are.

GLINDA. For reasons of safety I told you that my name is Gwin. G.W.N. I am Glinda the Witch of the North.

BEN. The good witch!

HARRY. From the Wizard of Oz!

GLINDA. Correct. Now, we all know who we are. Worry, you may begin.

WORRY. Thank you. As you all know, I have worried a great deal in the past year, hoping that good has come from evil. Cousin, you may interrogate the first witness.

OWL. Hoot. I call upon the Witch from Snow White.

WITCH FROM SNOW WHITE. (*Takes the "stand," angrily.*) Yes!

OWL. Hast thou dropped this nonsense about being the fairest of them all?

WITCH FROM SNOW WHITE. (*Shouts.*) I *am* the fairest of them all . . . (*Her attitude shifts suddenly. She purrs.*) that is, it simply doesn't matter to me any more. Further, I have been most kind to dear Snow White.

OWL. Snow White, is this the truth, forsooth?

SNOW WHITE. I'm afraid not. There has been no change that I can see.

OWL. Witch, the case is closed on your toes.

WITCH FROM SNOW WHITE. (*Grasps one foot.*) Ooooow!

Owl. Further punishment will be decided. Step aside.
Witch from Snow White. Zounds! (*Moves to one side.*)
Owl. Your witness, Worry.
Worry. Next case, the Wicked Witch of the West.
Witch of the West. (*Takes the "stand."*) From the West, yes, but wicked no more, I assure.
Worry. Let us hope that we are hearing the truth. Dorothy of Kansas, tell us that what she says is true.
Dorothy. I'm afraid that I can't. The witch has pursued me always and tried to take my ruby slippers. She captures my little dog Toto and forces his rescue. I've seen no change.
Worry. The witch who lies as a whim feels a tightening of brim.
Witch of the West. (*Grasps the brim of her hat.*) Oooow!
Worry. Move out, please. We'll deal with you shortly. Your witness, Glinda.
Glinda. Thank you, Worry, and don't fret. Surely there has been improvement in someone here. Next case, Miss Rottenmeier. (Miss Rottenmeier *moves into position.*) What can you tell us of yourself, Miss Rottenmeier? Have you kept your promise to us?
Miss Rottenmeier. What promise? Oh, promise! Of course I have, haven't I, Heidi!
Heidi. I'm afraid not, Miss Rottenmeier.
Miss Rottenmeier. Ungrateful child!
Heidi. I'm sorry, Miss Rottenmeier.
Miss Rottenmeier. Not as sorry as you're going to be. To bed without any supper! Uh, I mean, that is . . .
Glinda. Yes?
Miss Rottenmeier. I've helped her with her lessons, given her beautiful dresses, and loved her as my very own. Haven't I, Heidi!

HEIDI. Yes, Miss Rottenmeier.

GLINDA. Can it be true, at last?

MISS ROTTENMEIER. Tell her, Heidi. Tell her!

HEIDI. Yes. No! I say yes because she frightens me, even now.

GLINDA. As I suspected. Miss Rottenmeier, what do you say to that?

MISS ROTTENMEIER. I say rubbish!

GLINDA. And rubbish it shall be then. Can you smell it?

MISS ROTTENMEIER. (*Holds her nose.*) Ooooh! (*Staggers to the side.*)

GLINDA. Owl, your witness.

OWL. Hoot. King Midas take the stand.

KING MIDAS. (*Moves Center.*) I am pleased to report that I am the truly good one here. I have taken from the rich and given to the poor. In the past year I've kept nothing, absolutely nothing, for myself.

OWL. We're looking for improvement, King Midas, not a revolution. Robin Hood thee isn't. I sense untruth. Princess Tyra, have you been turned to stone in the past twelve divisions of the year?

PRINCESS TYRA. Oh, yes, Owl. Many, many times.

OWL. Then pockets of gold must turn to lead when such ridiculous lies be said.

KING MIDAS. (*Reels under sudden weight, moves heavily to one side.*) Ooooh!

WORRY. One more case and it's mine, unfortunately. Injun Joe, center. (INJUN JOE *moves into position.*) It would be hard for you to lie about your behavior after what we've already seen here today. We know that you haven't improved one smidgeon, but we need your testimony as to the true identity of the two boys before us. Do you know them?

INJUN JOE. This one Tom Sawyer. That one Huckleberry Finn.

HARRY. I'm not Tom Sawyer!

WORRY. Can you prove it?

HARRY. I don't know how.

WORRY. Very well, the case is settled. The court finds that you are Tom Sawyer and that your companion is Huckleberry Finn. Injun Joe, step aside. We'll deal with you later. Owl, please pass sentence on the boys.

OWL. Hoot. My boys, you are certainly not what this court would call villains, forsooth. However, you do bring grief and worry to Aunt Polly and to others who loves thee, who loves thee both.

HARRY. We really don't.

OWL. Thee thinks thee don't but thee do. Hast thee run away from home this year?

HARRY. Yes.

OWL. Hast thee?

BEN. Yes.

OWL. There, then. Case closed. Glinda, bring them the punishment. (GLINDA *exits*.) 'Tis true that this be your first time before us and your punishment shall be small.

WORRY. But punishment, nevertheless.

GLINDA. (*Returns with a paint can.*) Here it is. (*Places it on the ground before the boys.*)

WORRY. Pick up the container that you see before you. That's right, hold it up. You see, it has no bottom. It is the bottomless can of whitewash. The next time you trouble Aunt Polly you will paint the fence as punishment.

OWL. As always.

WORRY. The whitewash will fill to the brim and you will never see the bottom because there isn't one.

OWL. As you can readily see. Or not see.

BEN. But there's no whitewash in the can. Nothing at all.

WORRY. Not yet. Not until you are in trouble once more. And once full, the can will never be empty again.

GLINDA. Furthermore, we are giving you this sack full of treasures that you and your friends will enjoy. If you are good you will find it full of delightful surprises. If you are bad it will become a sack full of bricks.

BEN. What are the surprises?

GLINDA. Many things. Toys.

WORRY. Good books.

OWL. Ice cream money.

GLINDA. And other lovely surprises. If you are good.

BEN. And if not?

WORRY. A bag of bricks.

HARRY. We'll be good.

GLINDA. We shall see. We know that your intentions are good and that is a worthy beginning.

WORRY. The night grows dark. We must rest now.

OWL. Sweet shut-eye, long overdue.

WORRY. Yes, it's time for sleep.

HARRY. Sleep? Can't we go home now?

GLINDA. Not just yet. We have one more piece of business and we'll need your presence.

BEN. And then may we go?

GLINDA. Yes, you will be free to go home.

BEN. Home. I never thought I'd miss it so.

GLINDA. Then you've learned something of great value here already. Come, we must adjourn the meeting.

WORRY. The meeting is adjourned until morning.

OWL. Until sweet sleep we doth partake. (WORRY *yawns loudly.*) Uh, yes, exactly. Well put. Goodnight to one and all. (*Disappears from view.*)

WORRY. Goodnight all. Pleasant dreams. (*Disappears from view.*)

GLINDA. (*Claps her hands.*) Everyone to your sleeping places! (*Quietly everyone exits.* HARRY *and* BEN *are alone. They gather their belongings, the paint can, and the sack near them and pull their covers snug.*)

BEN. What a day this has been. Who will believe us when we tell them?

HARRY. We won't tell anyone. We'll keep it a secret.

BEN. And we'll have to be good. We don't want a bag of bricks.

HARRY. (*Yawns.*) We'll talk about it in the morning.

BEN. Agreed. (*They are asleep quickly.*)

(*The glen grows darker until* HARRY *and* BEN *are barely seen. The trees and shrubbery are little more than silhouettes. After a few moments the* WITCH OF THE WEST *tiptoes in from one side and crosses the glen. She stops and peers off intently. From another spot* INJUN JOE *sneaks in, stops, stares off in another direction, unaware of the* WITCH OF THE WEST. *The* WITCH FROM SNOW WHITE *enters from still another place and, unaware of the others, takes cover, staring off. Finally,* MISS ROTTENMEIER *enters, also unaware of the others, peers off in intense concentration. Slowly, all four inch backward toward* HARRY *and* BEN. *At a spot near the sack they bump each other, screeching in surprise and a chase begins in the darkness. One after another can be seen pursuing and being pursued. They chase in and out. Sometimes three chase one; sometimes one chases three. Finally, exhausted, all four drop in their tracks.*)

WITCH OF THE WEST. All right. Who gets that sack?

INJUN JOE. It's mine.

MISS ROTTENMEIER. Where is that written?

WITCH FROM SNOW WHITE. It is rightfully mine. It's full of juicy red apples.

ACT II   ON THE TIP OF MY TONGUE   41

MISS ROTTENMEIER. Where is *that* written?

WITCH OF THE WEST. It's full of ruby slippers!

MISS ROTTENMEIER. Nonsense. We'll have to admit it. There's nothing in that bag for us. It belongs to Tom Sawyer and Huckleberry Finn.

WITCH OF THE WEST. Ain't she noble, though.

INJUN JOE. She's right. No getting around it. Everyone sleep now. (*He rises, the others follow his lead.*)

WITCH FROM SNOW WHITE. Foiled again. Powerless to steal the sack.

WITCH OF THE WEST. For us it would be a bag of bricks. I don't want to fly that one back to Oz. Goodnight, wickeds. Have a good night . . . mare. Hahaa! (*Exits.*)

WITCH FROM SNOW WHITE. Have unpleasant dreams. (*Exits.*)

MISS ROTTENWEIER. Such rot. Ooooh. (*Holds her nose, exits.*)

INJUN JOE. (*To himself.*) No rest for the wicked. (*Exits.*)

(*The glen is still once more as the boys sleep on. After a moment there is a stirring in the bushes. KING MIDAS enters, tiptoes about to be certain that he is alone. He approaches the boys cautiously, takes the sack, opens it, reaches inside. Suddenly, the bag glows golden in the darkness.*)

KING MIDAS. Ah! A bag lined with gold and full of riches. At last! (*He closes the still glowing sack and prepares to leave, throwing the sack over his shoulder. He starts off. HARRY stirs, sits up.*)

HARRY. Who's there?

KING MIDAS. Nobody. Nobody here at all.

BEN. Harry, what is it?

HARRY. It's King Midas. He's taken our sack.

BEN. Look how it glows.

KING MIDAS. Is this *your* bag? I didn't know.

HARRY. Of course you knew. You were there when Glinda gave it to us.

KING MIDAS. (*Joins them.*) You're right, of course. I did know that. It's yours. (*Places it at their feet.*) I'm sorry.

HARRY. Won't you ever learn?

KING MIDAS. Oh, but I have learned. I wasn't taking the bag for myself. Truly.

BEN. Truly?

KING MIDAS. I swear it. You see, I've been called here so many times that I can't bear it any longer. I've finally learned that greed holds no reward.

BEN. But you were stealing our bag.

KING MIDAS. To give to the poor. When Owl Bird told me that I'm not Robin Hood it set me to thinking.

HARRY. That's all very nice but you were stealing, you'll have to admit.

KING MIDAS. Yes, I have to admit.

BEN. Were you really going to give to the poor?

KING MIDAS. I swear it. At last! But the bag is yours. I'll have to change in some other way.

HARRY. No! Take the bag.

KING MIDAS. What?

HARRY. Take it, it's yours, but swear that you won't keep it for yourself.

BEN. Yes, I agree to that. Take the bag, and swear.

KING MIDAS. My, oh, my, what generosity. I do. I do swear. The next time you read my story you'll see how I've changed. How pleased you will be. How pleased I am right now.

WORRY. (*Pops up as the light grows suddenly.*) At last! Everybody! Wake up! The miracle has happened! (*The glen is swiftly full of people as everyone returns.*)

ACT II ON THE TIP OF MY TONGUE   43

Owl. Hoot. Sweet sleep be short.

Worry. Who needs sleep at a time like this? Tell them Glinda.

Glinda. (*Claps her hands.*) Everyone! A miracle has occurred, we have been rewarded at last. There are honest and good intentions here tonight.

Witch of the West. Good intentions. Bah!

Glinda. It's a step in the right direction. It's all that we ask. The boys gave up their treasures for those who might need them more.

Injun Joe. Can't be true. Tom and Huck would never give away treasures.

Glinda. What you say is true. The boys have been telling us the truth all along. They are obviously not Tom and Huck. They truly are Harry Smith and Ben Jordan, the heroes of a brand new story and we are their supporting characters.

Harry. Then you believe us?

Glinda. We believe you and you are free. Not only have you done a noble deed in giving your bag full of treasures to someone else, you have helped to set King Midas on the road of good intentions.

Injun Joe. Could be just talk.

Glinda. It could be just talk, but we don't know that, do we? King Midas must have his chance.

Injun Joe. I read his story. Then I see.

Witch of the West. Can you read? Hahaaa!

Injun Joe. I learn, just to find out.

Glinda. You see? Even Injun Joe has good intentions. As for the rest, well, there's always next year.

Harry. Glinda, if Ben and I are the heroes of a brand new story, what is the story called?

Glinda. Oh, my, what is it called? Worry, do you know?

Worry. I did but I can't remember. Owl, do you know?

Owl. Zounds and Alackaday!

Worry. That's not the title.

Owl. Seems a classic title to me.

Worry. To you, it would, but it won't sell. I can nearly remember. I can nearly remember.

Glinda. I can nearly remember, too. It's . . . it's on the tip of my tongue.

Worry. On the Tip of My Tongue! That's it! Record it in the ledger, Owl!

Owl. Recorded. On the Tip of My Tongue!

Glinda. No, no! That wasn't the name of the story.

Owl. Recorded. Too late!

Glinda. In that case, so be it. On the Tip of My Tongue is the name of your story.

Snow White. And we're all in it.

Glinda. Yes, we are. It means that we have *all* taken a step in a new direction.

All. On the Tip of My Tongue! And we're in it!

Glinda. And now we must make the story end happily. Because the Wizard of Oz is not with us to give a heart, or a brain, or courage, I shall take his place. Gold medals will be awarded. First, to King Midas. (Midas *kneels to her.*) For discovering humility and for being the first villain in history to change his ways, the gold medal of the Grand Court of the Worry Bird.

King Midas. Thank you, Glinda. Though I may fail, I swear that I will try.

Glinda. I'm sure that you will not fail. Ben. (Ben *kneels to her.*) For being a good boy and for caring about those you left behind, your very own gold medal.

Ben. Thank you, Glinda. I promise to be good.

Glinda. Just do your best, Ben. Harry. (Harry *kneels to her.*) For being truly unselfish, for caring about others, and for becoming a beloved new hero, a gold medal and a happy ending.

ACT II   ON THE TIP OF MY TONGUE   45

HARRY. I'll do my best, I promise.

GLINDA. I know that you will. And now the trial has ended and the story is told. And Worry . . . don't worry.

WORRY. I won't. At least not as much.

GLINDA. To one and all, goodnight, and goodbye until we meet again. (*All wave goodbyes and exit. HARRY and BEN are alone once more.*)

HARRY. Ben, I have to sleep just a little before we go home. I've tried to sleep so many time, but I haven't gotten any rest.

BEN. Me, too. Besides, we'll need more light to find our way out of the glen.

HARRY. Just a short nap till morning.

BEN. I'll sleep well, I know. (*Once more, they pull their blankets about them. They are asleep quickly.*)

(*The light grows darker and darker as before. Dawn begins. Birds can be heard, and as the light builds morning bird songs build, also. The light grows slowly, slowly and music fills the glen. Now the sunlight is brilliant.*)

HARRY. (*Yawns, sits up, stretches, shakes BEN awake.*) Oooh, I slept so well.

BEN. Me, too. Let's go home, Harry.

HARRY. Home. What a wonderful word.

BEN. Breakfast.

HARRY. Mom.

BEN. My room.

HARRY. My bed. Ben, I'll never say ain't again.

WORRY. (*Pops up.*) What? What's this! Owl!

OWL. Hoot! Roused from a deep sleep before its time is spent!

WORRY. Stow the Shakespeare. This is serious.

OWL. Zounds!

WORRY. Who are these two? Do you know them? They're not on my list.

OWL. Lo and behold. I know not.

HARRY. We're Harry.

BEN. And Ben. Don't you remember us?

WORRY. How could I remember when we've never met?

HARRY. Home, Ben.

OWL. Post haste! You weren't invited!

HARRY. Home!

BEN. Home! (*They start to back out of the glen.*)

OWL. That's right! Home! Hurry, before you wake up.

BEN. Come on, Harry. (*They run from the glen.*)

OWL. Hurry home! Don't forget to wash the windows!

WORRY. Mow the lawn!

OWL. Paint the porch!

WORRY. Weed the garden!

OWL. Get thee to the store!

CURTAIN

PROPERTY LIST

PROLOGUE
    Paint can—Pre-set, on porch near door.
    Paint brush—Pre-set, with paint can.
    Paper money—Hildy.
    Grocery list—Hildy.

ACT ONE
    Cloth knapsack—Ben.
    Cloth knapsack—Harry.
    Apples—Pre-set, in Harry's knapsack.
    Blankets—Pre-set, one with each knapsack.
    Broom—Wicked Witch of the West.
    Wand—Glinda.
    Apple—Witch from Snow White.

ACT TWO
    Cage—Pre-set, containing Owl Bird.
    Cage—Pre-set, containing Worry Bird.
    Roll call scroll—Pre-set for Glinda, near Worry Bird.
    Bottomless paint can—Pre-set for Glinda, offstage.
    Brocade treasure sack—Pre-set for Glinda, offstage.
    Battery light—Pre-set in treasure sack for King Midas.

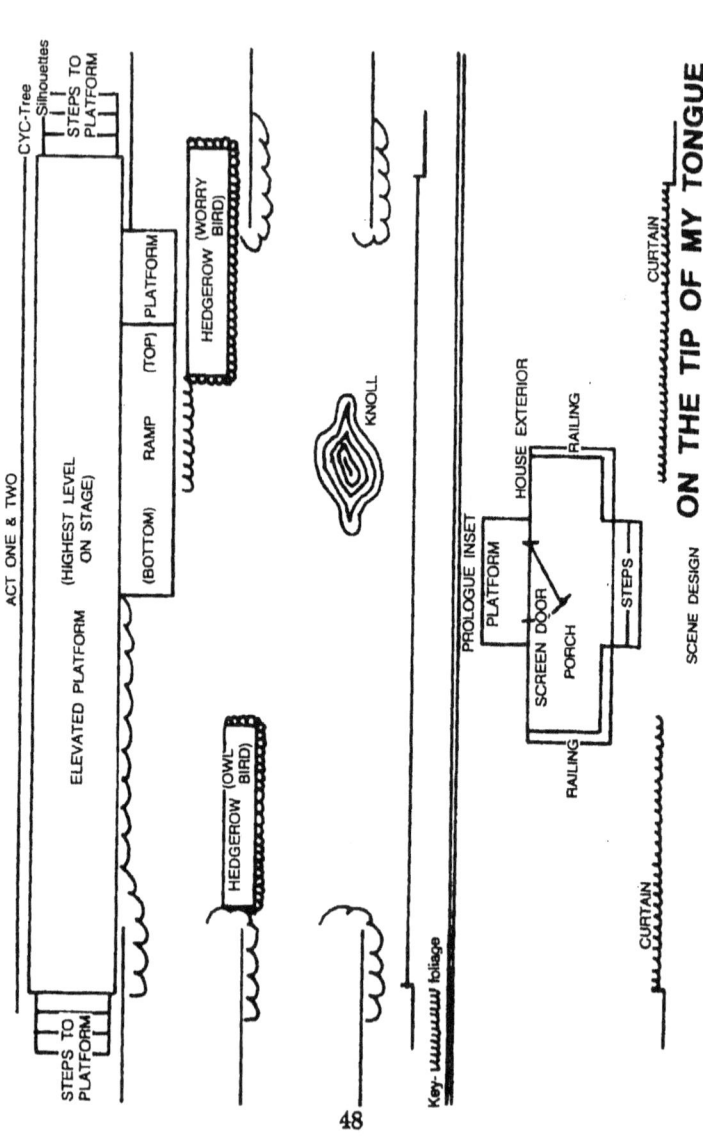

OTHER TITLES AVAILABLE FROM SAMUEL FRENCH

DANGER- GIRLS WORKING
James Reach

Mystery Comedy / 11f / Unit Set

At a New York girl's boarding house, there is a newspaper woman who wants to write a novel, a wise cracking shop girl, the serious music student, a faded actress, a girl looking for romance, the kid who wants to crash Broadway and other boarders. The landlady, is the proud custodian of the "McCarthy Collection," a group of perfect uncut diamonds. When it disappears from the safe, the newspaper woman is given two hours to solve the case before the police are called. Suspicion is cleverly shifted from one to the other of the girls and there's a very surprising solution.

SAMUELFRENCH.COM

OTHER TITLES AVAILABLE FROM SAMUEL FRENCH

MURDER AMONG FRIENDS
Bob Barry

Comedy thriller / 4m, 2f / Interior

Take an aging, exceedingly vain actor; his very rich wife; a double dealing, double loving agent, plunk them down in an elegant New York duplex and add dialogue crackling with wit and laughs, and you have the basic elements for an evening of pure, sophisticated entertainment. Angela, the wife and Ted, the agent, are lovers and plan to murder Palmer, the actor, during a contrived robbery on New Year's Eve. But actor and agent are also lovers and have an identical plan to do in the wife. A murder occurs, but not one of the planned ones.

"Clever, amusing, and very surprising."
– *New York Times*

"A slick, sophisticated show that is modern and very funny."
– WABC TV

SAMUELFRENCH.COM

OTHER TITLES AVAILABLE FROM SAMUEL FRENCH

VERONICA'S ROOM
Ira Levin

Thriller / 2m, 2f / Interior

This chilling mystery thriller by the author of *Rosemary's Baby* explores the thin line between fantasy and reality, madness and murder. Students Susan and Larry find themselves as guests enticed to the Brabissant mansion by its dissolute caretakers, the lonely Mackeys. Struck by Susan's strong resemblance to Veronica Brabissant, long- dead daughter of the family for whom they work, the older couple gradually induce her to impersonate Veronica briefly to solace the only living Brabissant, her addled sister who believes Veronica alive. Once dressed in Veronica's clothes, Susan finds herself locked in the role and locked in Veronica's room. Or is she Veronica, in 1935, pretending to be an imaginary Susan?

"Like being trapped in someone else's nightmare...jarring and (with a) surprising climax...a neat, elegant thriller."
– *Village Voice*

SAMUELFRENCH.COM

OTHER TITLES AVAILABLE FROM SAMUEL FRENCH

THREE YEARS FROM "THIRTY"
Mike O'Malley

Comic Drama / 4m, 3f / Unit set

This funny, poignant story of a group of 27-year-olds who have known each other since college sold out during its limited run at New York City's Sanford Meisner Theater. Jessica Titus, a frustrated actress living in Boston, has become distraught over local job opportunities and she is feeling trapped in her long standing relationship with her boyfriend Tom. She suddenly decides to pursue her dreams in New York City. Unbeknownst to her, Tom plans to propose on the evening she has chosen to leave him. The ensuing conflict ripples through their lives and the lives of their roommates and friends, leaving all of them to reconsider their careers, the paths of their souls and the questions, demands and definition of commitment.

SAMUELFRENCH.COM

OTHER TITLES AVAILABLE FROM SAMUEL FRENCH

TAKE HER, SHE'S MINE
Phoebe and Henry Ephron

Comedy / 11m, 6f / Various Sets
Art Carney and Phyllis Thaxter played the Broadway roles of parents of two typical American girls enroute to college. The story is based on the wild and wooly experiences the authors had with their daughters, Nora Ephron and Delia Ephron, themselves now well known writers. The phases of a girl's life are cause for enjoyment except to fearful fathers. Through the first two years, the authors tell us, college girls are frightfully sophisticated about all departments of human life. Then they pass into the "liberal" period of causes and humanitarianism, and some into the intellectual lethargy of beatniksville. Finally, they start to think seriously of their lives as grown ups. It's an experience in growing up, as much for the parents as for the girls.

"A warming comedy. A delightful play about parents vs kids. It's loaded with laughs. It's going to be a smash hit."
– *New York Mirror*

SAMUELFRENCH.COM

www.ingramcontent.com/pod-product-compliance
Lightning Source LLC
Chambersburg PA
CBHW070650300426
44111CB00013B/2358